Skeletons and Wine

by

Jason Kynge

For my love Renee without her none of this would be possible

First Edition: December 2017
Printed in the United States of America
ISBN-13: 978-1-948339-78-0

Life led Jason Kynge on a path of self discovery after like most he found himself having to find a way to heal a broken heart and troubled mind. Starting a Facebook page with the encouragement of other writers he began to share his innermost thoughts and heartfelt words.

Known for his raw honesty he appeals to those who have not only been where he is but to those who admire and appreciate a man who speaks from the heart. Not afraid to fall in love and write about it and even less afraid to write about the heartache of lost love and broken trusts.
Moments of cynicism and an honest evaluation of the world around him, often resonates as truth to those who find his words scrolling down their news feeds. Writing what others feel yet struggle to express with words, he has become a fearless voice in the truth of emotions for many.
Kynge's approach to writing is to speak his truth. You will never hear him claim to be an author or a poet yet this is exactly what he is. Through his words he grows, learns and sometimes crashes but he willingly brings you along for the journey.

Preface

Jason Kynge takes to a new platform in his first ever book. Not one to concern himself with the opinions of others when it comes to style or rules, Jason pens his words as only he can, full of passion and the truth as he knows it. Perhaps with a spelling or grammatical error here and there he takes to self-publish his first book. A book that reflects the learning, observations and growth of the average man who is far from average.

It is not possible to read each word and not find yourself falling in love with this man who has no problem opening his heart and making it visible to the world even at the risk of criticism.

A collection of writings from the Madman, the Hopeless Romantic and the Cynic. A journey full of past skeletons, lessons learned, new adventures and the wine it took to drown them out or write them down.

It is a beautiful thing to
not feel so alone in the
world.

To know so many
understand.

It is also devastatingly
heartbreaking, to know so
many understand.

-Jason Kynge

BEDTIME STORIES

Not everything you do will speak to everyone
Not everything you do will matter to all
Maybe only a few
But for those few it could the very thing that keeps them going another day
Not everything you do will be important to everyone
And that's okay
Because it's all important to you
(Things I tell myself at night when the world is quiet)

COFFEE KISSES

Life is too short for cheap coffee

Stale conversations

And passionless sex

So buy the gourmet

Discuss the universe and unicorns

And make love as if your life depends on it

Because it does

BLURRED VISION BLUES

I often stand in front of the mirror

Dissecting all the flaws I see

After a few drinks I'll come back to the same mirror

And think

You beautiful son-of-a-bitch

THE BIRD

Stop complicating life
Do as many shots of tequila as you can
And dance on that table
Find someone you like and get naked and sweaty
Find the joy flipping the middle finger can bring
Eat raw cookie dough for dinner
Stand at the edge of a cliff
Scream until your eyes water
If someone doesn't recognize your worth
Walk away
With your eager middle finger
Joyously in the air
Life isn't that complicated
People are just too afraid to let it be simple

HIT WITH A BIBLE

She asked me, "Why do you have so many issues

with religion?"

I told her one of the main reasons is too many

Are more concerned with what happens after this

life

Instead of how they treat people during this life

NEED A TISSUE

"What kind of person are you?"

"I'm the kind that says bless you to my cat when it sneezes, I feel like this tells you everything you need to know."

LOVE LANGUAGE

Words aren't always needed or necessary to say
I love you
Tell her in the way you kiss her
Tell her by the way you hold her hand in a crowd
Tell her in the way you cover her up at night
Pull her close
Tell her with the smile you wear
As she dances around the room
Tell her you love her daily without ever saying a
word

LABEL MAKER

She is wild
She is that spirited bohemian dancing in the rain
Smiling
She is chaos
Tempest
Unapologetic Aphrodite
My inamorata
A fierce shield maiden that wears her scars with
pride
She fought hard and earned every damn one
She is....
Actually who am I to place labels?
She is whatever the fuck she chooses to be today

SANDBOX

Adults complicate life to the point living becomes a
chore

A child gravitates to what makes them happy

They avoid what doesn't

It is this simple

EQUALS

Men run
Women run
Men change their mind or get scared
Women get scared or change their mind
Men like to feel appreciated
Women like to feel appreciated
Men love sex
Women love sex
Men lie
Women lie
Men play games
Women play games
Men need to feel safe
Women need to feel safe
We all want to feel valued as a person
It's all part of the human experience
It has nothing to do with what's between your legs

LIFE ON THE EDGE

Everyone claims to want a wild woman
Until they experience
Lying beside one they've angered
I for one have always found a twisted excitement
In not knowing if I will wake up the next day

LOVE UNCONDITIONALLY

I think this is a dangerous way to love
You will end up accepting things you should not
Yes keep hurting me
I love you unconditionally
Yes I know you slept with someone else
I love you unconditionally
Damn that
I have conditions
If you are incapable or unable
To give me your best
To put effort in
To be there with me as I learn and grow
To let me know I matter to you
I will wholeheartedly pack your bags and bolt the door

TAKING ME TO SCHOOL

"You will meet people during your life that are more in love with their fear, than they will ever be with you."

(Lessons my mother taught me)

PATIENCE

Someone is going to walk into your life
It's going to be unexpected
That's how it works
I beg of you don't compare
You're going to want to
I know
I find myself there
They say you only get that one love
One time
I believe this
That's the point
You were meant to learn what you could
From the last one
To help you grow
Now you're different

Changed

It's time for a new type of love

Maybe one that stays

The one you're finally ready for

Remember

It's going to be different

As it should be

Embrace it

Run with it

It may just be the adventure

You've been waiting for

CALL MY NAME

I've been a husband
Boyfriend
Shoulder
Distraction
Rebound
Late night text
Six shots of whiskey and I'm still an asshole
Dirty secret
I've been a great friend
Once or twice a soul mate
I'm not really sure what I want but I really like you
I've been this too
From the fuck me harder
To the take it slow
I've been
I wish we could go back and try again
Once I was
I'm going to marry you one day
I've been many things
But never have I been
Let me hold you
You're safe
You're home

WATCHTOWER

You looked at her but you didn't see her
See that she had magic coursing through her body
You ignored her heart
The one filled with fire
She could've been your arsonist
You only brought her tears
Tried to water her down
You didn't kiss her on the back the way she loves
You only ever turned yours away
You made her feel all alone in a crowded room
Now
I feel the voodoo in those fingertips
I stoke the fire that is her
If she views the world through watery eyes
It's from joy
I kiss her on the small of her back
And on those lips
My hand always finds hers in a sea of people
Reminding her she is safe
You looked
But didn't see
I didn't make that mistake

KAMIKAZE HEART

You go all in completely don't you?
Love hard?
I couldn't help but smile at this
Caution can be useful in some areas of life
That rickety old bridge you have to cross
Late night walks down a dark street
Swimming in rough seas
But not love
Never with love
I've been on the receiving end of half-assed
I've tasted lukewarm
You can have it
I want all in
I want a heart that is ready for cliff jumping
Fire walking
Climbing Everest
Ready for adventure
My heart is a kamikaze
It will crash into you with everything I am

SHOT OF CYNICISM

It wasn't my plan to become so damn cynical

But now when I hear

I love you

Aimed at me

I think

Why?

And

How long?

STURDY TABLE

I'm a gentleman
But if you keep looking at me like that
Biting your lower lip with the devil in your eyes
We are fucking against the nearest surface I can find

PILLOW MINTS

Hotel rooms have always felt strange to me
They have a way of reminding me of past lovers
I come in carrying my bags
I kick off my boots
Maybe jump on the bed and play
I put my toothbrush out
Put my clothes away
But I know it's temporary
Eventually I will have to leave
This isn't my home
And the longer I stay
The more I'll pay
So I pack up
I hit the road again
Someone has to clean up after me
They make the bed
Wipe down the counters
Remove the trash
Replace the mint on the pillows
It is as if I was never there
Now it's ready for the next guest

HEART THE SIZE OF FOREVER

She nudges me in the middle of the night
I roll over
Then I feel her wrap her arms around me
Pulling me in tight
This is new
Foreign
I've never been the one to be held before
Here is this woman
Her head stops at my chest
Yet she can bring me to my knees with just a look
I would go to war for her without hesitation
My life for her life without question
Yet here she is
In this moment
Reminding me that I too am watched over and protected
All I can do is smile
She may be no bigger than a minute
But her heart
Her heart is the size of forever

LIFE

I do not have the slightest clue what I'm doing
That's the adventure in it
I stopped worrying about it
That's the beauty of it

REFLECTIONS

I watched a man die once
He wasn't necessarily a loathsome person
Could he have been more loving?
Of course
Did he always make the best decisions?
Absolutely not
He drank too much
Didn't consider others feelings as he should have
He usually left a trail of destruction in his wake
Some even called him a complete bastard
They just never knew him like I did though
He didn't really mean to be careless with others
He was just fighting his own demons
He always knew he could be more than he was
I suppose you could say it was because he was never taught how to achieve that
This is why he failed so many times
But that isn't really an excuse

The day finally arrived when something had to be done
Pain that he had caused couldn't be allowed to continue
It was time for him to go
I saw the tears in his eyes
I saw the word sorry form on his cheeks
I can't tell you he went peacefully with no pain
That would be a lie
Death is never easy even when it's necessary
So I watched him go
I said my goodbye to this man I had always known
Stared him straight in the eyes
Then I walked away from the mirror

CHECKLIST

If you're struggling in a relationship I want you to
ask yourself three question
Do they understand me
Do they try to understand me?
Do I still feel their love even when they don't
understand me?

Answer these honestly
Act accordingly

FUNERAL PYRE

I honestly don't know what will happen when I close
my eyes on this life
My lack of faith tells me nothing
I suppose I will find out in due time
It is the reason I live as I do
The cornerstone of my own belief system
Make the most of now
Love fiercely
Be loved the same
Travel as often as possible and talk to strangers
Soak in the day to day
Laugh and play
Cuddle hard
Fuck the same
Dance in the kitchen
Dance in the rain
Everything has an expiration date
This is something none of us can escape
No I don't have any idea what will happen when my
time is up
All I know without any doubt
Is I will make every moment of my life count

MESSY

Do not confuse life and love
Life will get difficult
The bills never stop
Stress will threaten to strangle
Jobs are going to get old and feel like they are sucking out your soul
You will cry
You will get angry
You will have days you question just what the hell it is you're doing because you honestly don't have a damn clue
Then there will be the days you bask in glorious numbness
Cars will break down
You may find that you must gather possessions to sell
The dinner menu may consist of grilled cheese sandwiches every single night
Most days you will only live on hope
That is life
It gets messy and chaotic
Too many associate the chaos with love
That the mess gets hard so love must be hard
Love isn't hard
Love is a blanket on a lazy Sunday curled up with a cup of coffee and a kiss
Love is what makes it all worthwhile

SOLITUDE

How do you live with someone that is never wrong?

You don't

You let them be right

Alone

Without you

ZIPPED LIPS

If they won't claim you in public

They haven't earned the right

To say I love you

In private

STRANGERS

If we ever meet again it will be as strangers
You haven't met this new me
I have changed
The way I view the world has changed also
I see things differently now
I see you differently
You will look at me but no longer recognize the person staring back at you
One of the most beautiful parts of this transformation
I no longer give a fuck how I look to you

GLASS SLIPPER

If there is evil in the world
Far greater than any fairytale
Take heart
For this means there is love
More extraordinary as well

GRANDFATHER CLOCK

Such a strange thing
We always think we have time
Time to go visit
Time for a hug
Time to make new memories
But there always comes a time
When we have to say goodbye
Even if we aren't ready

PUZZLE PIECE

I love you
And I don't know what to do with myself
I love you
And the world is so much smaller without you
I love you
And I'm afraid you don't love me as fiercely as I do you
I love you
Because you strangle my fears when I start to think like that
I love you
For the way you slide over to me and put your head on my chest
I love you
For the way your skin feels on mine
I love you
Because when I'm down or struggling you lift me up and I do the same
I love you
Because you let me

I love you
Because despite all the obstacles and struggles we still choose each other day in and day out
I love you
For the way your lips bend and your hips dance
I love you
For the way you make me feel safe and desired
I love you
For the rhythm of your words and the flow of your body
I love you
For the way you love me

BANANAS

We like to tell ourselves we've evolved as a species
Yet we still massacre one another over which loving
religion is the correct one
Still quarrel and kill over a stranger's skin tone
Objectify and demean one another based off of
reproductive organs
Our technology has advanced
Humanity just hasn't caught up
We are apes with itchy trigger fingers

LETTING GO

I'll tell you a secret
Every strong woman that has to always be in control
That feels like they have to be in charge of others during the day
At work
In life
Craves a savage to pin her to a wall
Put your hands around her neck and kiss her deep
Guide her to the bed or bend her over the nearest surface
Throw her over your shoulder if necessary
Rip those panties off and devour her
Let her be free
Help her to let go
Take control
Put your hands around her wrist and fuck her like you mean it
Let her for that moment feel small
Create a safe place for her demons and fears to come out and play
Swallow them whole
Slap her ass and grip her hips like you mean business
If you give her space to release all she holds inside
She will love you as only fierce and wild things can

SPLINTER

I think there are some of us

We have been searching our entire lives

Like we are expecting at any moment

To stumble across something magical

I think that is part of our restlessness

We know something

We feel it

We just aren't sure what it is

WORTH THE RISK

Hurt is the risk we all take
I let you in you may make a mess of things
Even if you're scared
If you aren't willing to risk it all you will never know how deep love can go
If you aren't willing to take the chance what are you doing here?
Wasting time?
Simply existing?
You get one go around in life
Stop living it in fear of what may happen and get excited about what could happen
Life is unpredictable
This is part of the adventure
You owe it to yourself to see what is out there

Could your choices crash and burn?
Fuck yes they could
Nothing is guaranteed
Those choices could also end up leading you to the most beautiful moments of your life
So get off your ass and face these fears
Stop wasting your time scared of a what-if
Start making it all count
Tomorrow may very well be your last day
Live and love each one like it is

FOOT RUBS AND DOING THE DISHES

So she's a little cynical

Be willing to try harder

Have a desire to learn everything about her

Also be prepared for her good days and bad

So she's a little jaded

Give her a reason to finally not be

BEHAVE YOUR WORDS

Stimulating conversation with a beautiful woman is
frankly one of the most seductive things
Lingerie will never hold a candle to a woman that
can melt your mind with her words

PERFECTLY IMPERFECT

She worries about her belly
That perhaps it's too big or has stretch marks or this or that
Her insecurities sometimes threaten to eat her alive
Part of my job in loving her is to consume those fears
To push her knees up to her chest and kiss every inch of her
To run my hands and lips across that stomach
Let her know that to me she is perfect
Not just because of how she looks on the outside
But more importantly because of who she is as a person and for the way she loves me with all that she is

RICH

I didn't win the lottery today
But I made her smile
Bills continue to roll in
She held my hand today
I couldn't find the right words today
She told me that she loves me
I was plagued with doubt in myself
She held me in her arms until it was silent
The world exhausted me today
She snuggled up to me and kissed me
There are many ways to be rich in life
If we know how to look

SELFIE

In the age of dick pics
Reality television
I'm right you're wrong
You hurt me so now I hurt you
This happened in the past so let me show you what
it feels like so in another fifty years we can switch
and repeat and you can show me
Unplug
Go sit by the sea
Just look and listen
Go into the woods
Sit by a fire
Drink hot chocolate and let the sounds of nature talk
to you
With a loved one or all alone
Sometimes revolutions can be quiet
Sometimes being a revolutionary means walking
away from all the bullshit

WAKE UP

Some people see things changing

All I see is the same cycle wrapped in new packaging

Run by the same people it has always been

Some people see change

I see us making the same mistakes going nowhere

quickly

We want things to be different

We just don't want to do them differently

We want to change the dream

Speak of being

Woke

All I see is humanity sleep walking off a cliff

YOU'RE SNORING

Every relationship goes through phases
I think maybe my favorite is what comes after the honeymoon
The one where things get real and you don't tiptoe
The part where you are in the shower and the other one burst in to pee
Where you stop worrying about always looking a certain way and the relationship pants come out
You know the ones
Maybe they have some holes or rips but damn if they aren't the most comfortable things
The phase where you can sit in silence and still be perfectly content and you aren't bothered by the silence or the need to constantly entertain
The phase where you accidentally or intentionally fart and then just grin
I love when it gets real

SOMETHING REAL

To the fathers doing it alone
Learning how to be mothers also
To the men who come home smelling of grease and sweat and the loss of youthful dream`s
Exhausted from the day`
May we never have to walk a day in your steel toe boot`s
To the ones who grew up without fathers of their own doing their best to navigate what it means to be man
While paying for the sins of those that came before
To those that cry at night hidden away from judging eyes because men aren't supposed to weep but sometimes life gets overwhelming
As you battle within yourself telling your heart to stop watering your eyes but you also just want to be held and be told
Everything is going to be okay
To the ones that hide a fountain of emotion and if someone would just dig a little deeper they'd never thirst again

To the ones playing catch because they know what it is like to throw the ball alone
To the ones that love to play and be silly if only they were made to feel comfortable enough to know that side of them is in safe hands
To the ones standing in front of the mirror judging themselves off of unrealistic expectations
Worried they'll never be loved because their stomach isn't hard enough or their arms big enough or for the fact they don't stand tall enough
To the ones too afraid to speak up or out about pain they`ve experienced because the tough men just deal with it silently
To the ones that make you laugh
To the ones with an ocean heart waiting desperately for the one ready to swim
Good men aren't a myth
They aren't unicorns
They are out there right now
Waiting to be seen
Ready for someone to believe

BE WILLING

We all have the ability to help someone become the best version of who they are

Lift them up

We all have the potential to guide those we love to be more

But it requires us to be more

This is why so many things fail

Sometimes it is easier to see what another person is lacking

Instead of looking at what we are adding

BIRTH

I don't think any of us are unique
We all deal with the same feelings at some point in our life
I believe the only thing that separates us is what we choose to do with those emotions
And those decisions are where either a monster
Or a unicorn
Is born

CRIMSON SATURDAY

It`s November
Thanksgiving to be precise
I didn't celebrate the holiday
In fact I rarely celebrate holidays anymore
With the exception of New Year`s Eve and St.
Patrick's Day
I love anything that comes with a drink
Even more so if it is followed by a kiss
I never have really understood celebrating
Thanksgiving anyway
I always imagine that is was drearier than my old
books painted it
The first one
It`s cold and I am sitting on my front porch smoking
My stomach is in pain
I ate too many hot wings
To Hell with a turkey
I am willing to bet people are shivering standing in
some long line outside right now

Ready to step on the backs of one another when
those doors swing open
Approved of riots
Everyone grab whatever you can as quickly as you
can
Reminds me of a picture I saw once of
Hundreds of sheep trying to squeeze through this
little narrow little gate
It looked like they had been pinched in the middle
then fanned out once they were through it
Except there was no fence
It was completely open
Just a gate
I don't have a desire to celebrate any of this
My love is waiting in bed
Our bed
With a glass of wine and a soft touch
Now this is something worth celebrating
And the best part
I get to do it again tomorrow

MORE THAN A WORD

I've written about home many times

I'm going through my clothes to fill a suitcase
Smelling shirts to see what should go in the wash
Folding those that I feel are tolerable

I've written about home many times

Do I have my toothbrush?
Maybe I'll just buy a new one when I get to where I'm going
Hairbrush?
Deodorant?
Just toss it all in

I've written about home many times

I pause to go make coffee in the now familiar kitchen
Listen to gurgling sound of it brewing while I grab the bottle of baileys to top it off

I've written about home many times

I'm just going to go sit on the porch for a moment
Enjoy my coffee with a cigarette in my favorite chair
Listen to the neighbors chit-chat as they walk their dog

I've written about home many times

I go back in to finish putting my things in the bag
There's her wine glass sitting on the table
A tube of lip balm because she is addicted to having soft lips
I'm addicted to those soft lips
Her nightgown is on the bed
The one that hugs her just right and the strap is always running away from her shoulder
Exposing just enough flesh to drive me wild

I've written about home many times

The heavy feeling in my chest makes me painfully aware that before now home was just a word
Spoken about with youthful ignorance

I've written about home many times

Now it will feel strange sleeping in a bed that isn't my own
Alone
Maybe I'll cover some pillows with a blanket and just pretend that feeling beside me is you

Home is just a word until that person comes along and gives it true meaning

CONFESSIONS

I put a lot on my shoulders and I want to aim high
But then self-doubt kicks in
And I'm afraid to try
Because what if I do
What if I believe
What others say?
I try
And I fail
I'll look like a fool
Maybe not to you
But to me
I get so scared that I just want to run and hide
I'll keep all these dreams locked deep inside
Because at least there they are always beautiful
There I'm successful and accepted and doing well
Locked away I didn't fail
Or did I
I wish I knew where these feelings come from
From what shore they sail
Across what sea

Why can't I see?
Maybe for a day I could borrow your eyes
Would it all look different?
Would it be like I was baptized and I'll arise a new man and wise
Or
Can I just start to love myself?
Without the need for approval
Without this crippling fear that forces me to crawl
because if I run I may trip
Fall
I hold back so much because I'm terrified that what I have to give falls short of the mark then who am I if you reject me do I cease to exist
No
I just have to repeat this over and over until I know
Let go of the pressure
Diamonds aren't rare and I'm only human
This is all I have to be
So when fear creeps in and doubt tags along
And when I think I'm about to begin
Believing what it's selling

And telling me I won't stack up
That it will all crash and burn
And I should just hang it up
Stop
I will never be perfect
Even if I found perfection in the end
I would need to flaw it up
Because it's those things that make life beautiful
Those little moments and people with a few cracks
That live well enough to be called maniacs
Keep life interesting
And if I can see their beauty
Maybe I can learn to see my own
I'll admit I'm still afraid
But I need to stop looking at it as I could fail
And remember I'm always just learning
And if something doesn't work the first time

Turn the page

Kynge

68725638R00038

Made in the USA
San Bernardino, CA
07 February 2018